This eturned on or before
.....ped below.

THE VICTORIAN WOMAN

THE VICTORIAN WOMAN

Suzanne Fagence Cooper

V&A Publications

First published by V&A Publications, 2001

V&A Publications
160 Brompton Road
London SW3 1HW

Designed by Bernard Higton

ISBN 1851773304

A catalogue record for this book is available from the British Library

Printed in Singapore

Jacket illustrations:
Front: James Tissot, *Hush – the Concert* (detail). See plate 49.
Back: *Hindhaugh's Wholemeal.* Poster. V&A: E.24-1973.

Frontispiece: *The Newest French Fashions Modelled for the Young
Englishwoman.* Fashion plate for Ward, Loch & Tyler, 1873.
V&A: BGM Library.

V&A Publications
160 Brompton Road
London, SW3 1HW
www.vam.ac.uk

CONTENTS

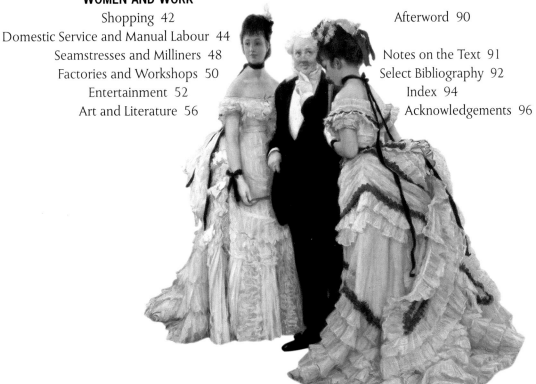

INTRODUCTION

Most of us have a fixed image of a Victorian woman. We think of her, encumbered by her corsets and crinolines, struggling feebly against the confinement of the domestic sphere. She reminds us conveniently of a caged songbird, admired for her ornamental qualities, but largely useless.

Recently we have been asked to reassess our perception of the women of the nineteenth century. Our expectations seem to be undermined by the image of the Pre-Raphaelite seductress, or by photographs of mill-girls and housemaids that demonstrate the importance of working women to the Victorian economy. Then there are the tales of sexual double-standards, prostitution and outcast single mothers. In fact, we build up a picture of several very different sorts of Victorian women – the domestic angel in conflict with the working woman and the street-walking whore. We also have to come to terms with the image of Queen Victoria herself, Empress of India, ruling over millions of poor working women, who were themselves unable to exercise political power.

These contradictions were visible to the Victorians. They too struggled to reconcile the ideal of motherhood and domesticity with the harsh realities of poverty and the need to earn a living. This book tackles three themes in an attempt to make sense of these contradictions. Firstly, it considers the myths surrounding womanhood in this period, and compares them with the experiences of the women who lived through it. This section focuses on the example of the Queen, as dutiful wife, mother and widow. Secondly, it looks at the various types of employment that were available to women. Many families faced a constant battle with poverty in which wives and daughters played their part as wage-earners. The third section maps the changes in women's roles from the 1860s, with new scope for work, leisure and travel. This final section deals with those women who broke the boundaries of convention, and in doing so broadened the fields of activity that were open to women. During her long reign, Victoria witnessed dramatic changes in the status of women. By considering this diversity of experience, we can perhaps achieve a greater sympathy with the Queen and her female subjects.

1 (opposite). Roger Fenton, *Queen Victoria and Prince Albert*. Photograph, 1854. V&A: 113-1947

MYTH AND REALITY

THE ANGEL IN THE HOUSE

In 1854 the English poet Coventry Patmore (1823–94) published *The Angel in the House*, describing an idealised courtship. Over the course of the century, his ideal Angel grew out of all proportion to the descriptions of Honoria, the heroine of the poem, and the term came to be applied to every demure wife who created a haven for her menfolk in the well-ordered home.

Her image seemed so all-pervasive that she fell foul of the anti-Victorian backlash of the mid-twentieth century. Virginia Woolf, writing in 1942, described how, at the end of Victoria's reign, 'every house had its Angel. She was intensely sympathetic. She was immensely charming. She was utterly unselfish ... She sacrificed herself daily ... if there was a draught, she sat in it ... Her purity was supposed to be her chief beauty'.[1] Woolf defined the Angel as a repressed woman, who could not act outside her domestic sphere, whose only thought was for her family and who was free from the taint of sexual awareness.

The image of the devoted, home-loving Victorian woman was deep-rooted, but did she really exist? A journalist for the *Saturday Review*, writing in 1867, evidently thought that a man would be able to find 'the ideal of womanhood ... her husband's friend and companion, but never his rival; one who would consider their interest identical ... who would make his house his true home and place of rest ... a tender mother, an industrious housekeeper'.[2] This article presented the widely-held belief in 'separate spheres': the husband should go out into the world to earn enough to keep his wife at home, and she should be occupied with providing a cheerful domestic environment. In the model relationship, each partner had their own responsibility, and the wife's duties – educating the children, managing the household and providing emotional support for her husband – were not undervalued. However, the husband maintained his position as the head of the family.

This division of labour was presented in journalism and novels as the ideal for most of the century. Yet in many households it was an impossibility. For countless families, the wages earned by the wife and unmarried daughters were essential. This had always been the case, but in pre-industrial Britain women had often been able to work at home as part of the family business. In the textile industry, for example, women traditionally worked as spinsters, while their menfolk wove the wool on hand-looms, either at home or in a nearby house. With the establishment of large textile mills, employment moved out of the home and into the factory, and the role of women in the industry became a matter of controversy. Women could be employed at lower wages than men. As a result, one of the most common grievances among male workers was that female employees were taking jobs away from the natural breadwinners in the family, their husbands and fathers. In addition, there were fears that the long working hours and poor conditions

2. Julia Margaret Cameron, *The Angel in the House*. Photograph, 1873. V&A: E.2309-1997.

The idealised woman conjured up by Coventry Patmore became the inspiration for works of art, and, later, the butt of satire.

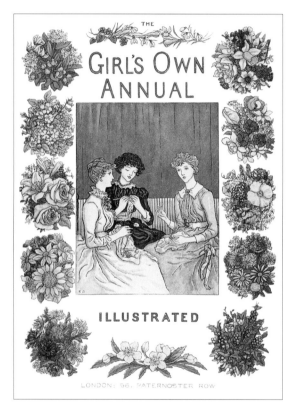

3. Kate Greenaway, *The Girl's Own Annual*. Book illustration, late 1870s. V&A: E.2436-1953.
Girls were encouraged to develop their skills in needlework, music and housekeeping, in order to help them create a cheerful domestic environment for their future husbands. The ideal young wife presented in *Punch* magazine declared 'I don't believe I have any mission beyond my own fireside.' (1853)

would have a deleterious effect on women with babies and young children.

From the mid-century, when *The Angel in the House* was written, the ability of a husband to keep his wife out of the workplace signified respectability, or a family's aspirations towards joining the growing ranks of the middle classes. The other symbol of respectable status, as Virginia Woolf recognised, was the protection of women from contact with sexual matters. Chaste daughters and a docile wife were the signs of a well-ordered household. This emphasis on sexual innocence was an ideal, rather than a reality, but it was founded on strongly-held beliefs about women's sexuality. Although many twentieth-century critics of the Victorians have stressed Dr William Acton's pronouncements of 1857 that 'The majority of women ... are not very much troubled with sexual feeling of any kind',[3] this attitude was in fact contradicted by many of his contemporaries. Most nineteenth-century theories of female sexuality, both medical and popular, emphasised the overwhelming potential for sexual arousal. Her latent eroticism was an essential part of the focus on woman as child-bearer. As one mid-century commentator explained, she could be so highly responsive to sexual arousal that 'a woman of sensibility, who would preserve her chastity, must guard her bosom well'.[4]

This belief in the heightened eroticism of the female body was expressed in descriptions of women as more feeling – and more easily swayed – than men. It was also closely linked to theories about conception. Until the 1880s, at least, women were encouraged to think that they could only conceive if they, too, had

4. Clementina, Lady
Hawarden, *Man at Window,
Girl in Chair*. Photograph,
c. 1861. V&A: PH.457-1968.
Middle-class respectability
was defined by maintaining
'separate spheres': 'man's
sphere, the world; woman's
sphere, the home' and 'each
exercised on the other a
most blessed influence.'
(*Punch*, 1853)

reached orgasm. James Copland's *Dictionary of Medical Practice* (1844–58) was clear about this: 'It is generally understood by females of all ranks in society, that indifference during intercourse, or suppression of the orgasm, will prevent impregnation, and although they are sometimes deceived in this respect, yet their inference is correct in the majority.'[5]

The combined weight of these theories makes it hardly surprising that Victorian wives could be fearful of sexual pleasure. It also helps to explain why fathers should wish to keep the smouldering sensuality of their daughters in check. Mr Podsnap, in Charles Dickens' novel *Our Mutual Friend* (1864–5), was only too aware of the capacity for excitement in his daughter, and tried as hard as he could to avoid subjects that 'could bring a blush to the cheek of the young person'. However, he was constantly dismayed to find that 'the soberest tints of drab, white, lilac and grey were all flaming red' in her eyes. Hence the desire to protect girls from the stimulation of encounters with sexual knowledge.

One way to counteract the apparent dangers of these heightened emotions was to present women as victims. The female body, weakened by monthly ebbs and flows, was in constant need of male protection. The artistic vogue for classical Andromedas, medieval damsels in distress and slave girls demonstrated this desire to display the erotic potential of women, and male responsibility to defend them.

Equally telling are the images of women whose passion broke the bounds of convention, and who became a danger to themselves or to others. The Lady of Shallot, heroine of Alfred, Lord Tennyson's poem of 1832, left her weaving to look out of her tower at Sir Lancelot, and brought a curse upon herself. She was driven to drift in a boat down to Camelot, singing softly, until 'her blood was frozen slowly, And her eyes were darkened wholly'. Her passion, and her refusal to remain demurely in her enclosure, caused her death.

In addition to all the other influences upon middle-class households, there was the powerful model of the royal family. Queen Victoria made no secret of her love for Prince Albert, and her letters and diaries were full of praise for his good looks and good sense. They were married on 10 February 1840 at the Chapel Royal, St James's Palace, London, almost two years after her coronation. In the 21 years of their marriage, she bore him 9 children. When the Prince Consort died, probably of typhoid, in December 1861, the Queen was prostrated with grief. She had relied upon her husband both emotionally and practically, to support her in her duties of government, and she set an example to women of all classes by her constant attachment to her family. Victoria managed to combine sovereign authority with a loving humility in the presence of her husband. As a result, it was the Queen who established the ideal figure of the Victorian wife and mother.

5. Charles Dodgson, *Kate Terry as Andromeda*. Photograph, 1865. V&A: Theatre Museum.

This photographer, more commonly known as Lewis Carroll, was reflecting a trend in Victorian art to present women as victims.

MOTHERHOOD

6. Leonida Caldesi and Montecchi, *The Royal Family on the Terrace at Osborne House*. Detail. Albumen print, 1857. V&A: 68.021. The Queen's first child, Princess Victoria, was born in November 1840, a mere nine months after her wedding. She bore eight more children, with Beatrice, the last, in 1857.

7. Waterlow family album, *Mother and Children*. Photograph, 1860s. V&A: 3809-1953. The long exposure times required for early photographs can give an impression of constraint. Only rarely was the spontaneous affection and excitement of family life captured.

With a woman as the head of state, the private acts of the royal family became intensely public, as the Queen passed through childbirth and mourned her husband. During the course of her reign, Victoria came to be seen as the 'Mother of the Nation' and the 'Mother of the Empire', and in her wake the position of women as the upholders of British morality and vitality was considerably enhanced.

For many working class women, however, motherhood only added to their difficulties. Of course they wanted to create a secure domestic environment for their husbands and children, but this could be well beyond their means. Chartist women in Newcastle-upon-Tyne wrote that 'for years we have struggled to maintain our homes in comfort, such as our hearts told us should greet our husbands after their fatiguing labours', but 'our wishes have no prospect of being realised, our husbands are

8 (above). Sir John Everett Millais, *Eliza Wyatt and her daughter, Sarah*. Oil on wood, *c*.1850. Tate Gallery, London.

The relationship between mother and child was consecrated in paintings that made deliberate parallels with Renaissance images of the Madonna.

overwrought, our houses are half-furnished, our families ill-fed and our children uneducated.'[6] If women went out to work to bring in sorely-needed wages, they had to find someone to mind their young children. In many families, a relative or neighbour could look after them, but there were other, less fortunate, arrangements, in which children were handed over to unscrupulous minders, who dosed them with laudanum and treacle, a mixture that 'keeping them quiet, prepares them for the silence of their impending grave.'[7]

MARRIAGE AND 'REDUNDANT WOMEN'

10. Clementina, Lady Hawarden, *Sisters at a Window – Isabella looking out, Clementina looking in.* Photograph, c. 1860. V&A: PH.267-1947.

Like Laura and Marion in Wilkie Collins' novel *The Woman in White,* many sisters dreaded the separation caused by marriage.

domestic and foreign policy. Secondly, it encouraged the hope that the young Queen would soon produce an heir to ensure the stability of the monarchy. Victoria's wedded bliss also distanced her from the scandals that surrounded the domestic arrangements of her Hanoverian predecessors.

Finding a husband was clearly a priority for many Victorian girls. Journalists, novelists, even the Queen herself were all conspiring to make marriage essential for any woman who wanted to live up to the ideals of domestic responsibility and motherhood. There were dissenting voices, but the expectation that a girl should marry prevailed. All levels of society that had any claim to respectability agreed that this should be the case. In 1851, for example, only 29 per cent of women over 20 years old were unmarried.

However, finding a suitable partner could be tricky. The Census of 1851 found that there were 500,000 more women in Britain than men. What was to be done with these so-called 'redundant women'? Some commentators feared that the surplus of single women was contributing to the visible growth in prostitution in the cities. One industrialist, W.R. Greg, suggested that the problem could be solved by encouraging these women to emigrate. His plan to 'remove five hundred thousand women from the mother country ... to the colonies' would serve two purposes: it would protect British men from

Queen Victoria's wedding was a far more significant event than her coronation in setting the tone for her reign. In the first place, it was clear from the outset that, unlike that other redoubtable queen, Elizabeth I, she would not use courtship as a bargaining tool in

11. *Bride, Bridesmaid and Child.* Fashion plate, 1870–72. V&A: E.2221-1988. The conventional white wedding was popularised by Queen Victoria's own celebrations. Marriage rates rose steeply from 1840 to the late 1860s, and barely slackened thereafter.

12 (right). Wedding gown. White silk gauze with lace trimming 1872. V&A: T.68F-1962.

predatory single women, and promote civilisation and white population growth in the settlements of Australasia and British North America.[8]

For those women who did not want to be shipped off to the colonies, there could be disadvantages in domesticity. Many girls of the upper and middle classes found that their freedom was severely reduced once they married. Their legal position was not necessarily improved as, until 1870, all goods and funds belonging to a wife automatically passed to her

husband upon marriage. During the later Victorian period a series of Acts of Parliament enabled women to take control of their own property. In 1870 it was agreed that a married woman could retain £200 of her own earnings, and in 1882 a new Act allowed married women to own and administer property.

A married woman was also at a disadvantage if it came to divorce. Until 1857 each divorce could only be obtained by an individual Act of Parliament, a process that was clearly beyond the means of most families. The Matrimonial Causes Act of 1857, which applied to England and Wales, enabled a husband to divorce his wife for adultery, but a wife could only divorce her husband if she could prove cruelty, desertion, incest, rape, sodomy or bestiality in addition to adultery. For most of Victoria's reign, a husband could also restrict his wife's access to her children, and insist that she fulfilled her conjugal duties.

There were other ways to escape an impossible relationship, as Effie Ruskin demonstrated when she obtained an annulment of her marriage to the art critic John Ruskin, on the grounds of non-consummation. However, separation from one's husband, by whatever means, guaranteed scandal.

Of course, many couples enjoyed the loving relationship that was represented in the ideal life of the royal family, but any marriage was an upheaval. In particular, it would often distance a woman from her family. Many women relied on the companionship of their sisters, and the intensity of these relationships was celebrated by poets, novelists and artists. Laura and Marion in Wilkie Collins' *The Woman in White* (1860) were only one example of a pair of sisters who dreaded the separation caused by marriage. Despite much encouragement, the expectation of domestic bliss was not shared by all Victorian women.

13 (opposite). Sir John Everett Millais, *Trust Me*. Oil on canvas, 1862. Forbes Magazine Collection.
Until 1882, a woman was still legally the 'chattel' of her husband, and could find that she lost a degree of independence when she left her father's house to marry.

14 (above). William Quiller Orchardson, *Mariage de covenance*. Oil on canvas, 1883. Glasgow Museums: Art Gallery and Museum, Kelvingrove.

The 'marriage market', where property was more relevant than affection, was analysed and exposed by artists and novelists. Anthony Trollope was particularly scathing in his novel *The Way We Live Now* (1873).

DEATH AND MOURNING

As the Queen was to discover on 14 December 1861, the happiest married life could be cut short by the death of a husband. Victoria was devastated by the loss of her Prince Consort, and devoted herself to mourning his memory. The Blue Room at Windsor, where he died, was left as a shrine, and the Queen slept with a wreath and a photograph of Albert on his deathbed above her pillow. She was overwhelmed by her duties, which, until now, she had shared with her husband. She wrote in despair 'He did everything – everywhere! *Nothing* did I do – without him – from the greatest to the smallest – from State Affairs – from Political Questions to ... the buying of a dress or bonnet ... *all* was done together; my first word was "I must ask Albert".'[9] Victoria continued to wear mourning until her own death, some 40 years later.

For many of her subjects, grief was only too common a feature in their lives. Alfred, Lord Tennyson captured the heart of the nation in his poem *In Memoriam* (1850), which charted the process of grieving and the struggle to hold onto religious belief:

I stretch lame hands of faith, and grope,
   And gather dust and chaff, and call
   To what I feel is Lord of all,
And faintly trust the larger hope.

Certain trades were notoriously dangerous, and wives of fishermen or miners had to face the prospect of losing their husband. Popular papers such as the *Illustrated London News* regularly

15 (left). Jet necklace, *c.* 1880.
V&A: M.994-1983.
The heavy mourning
costume adopted by the
Queen set a trend for other
widows and helped to create
a thriving jet carving
industry, based in Whitby.

16 (right). H.W. Brewer,
*Frogmore: Interior of the
Royal Mausoleum.*
Watercolour, 1869. The Royal
Collection, © HM Queen
Elizabeth II.
Queen Victoria ordered that
a private mausoleum should
be built at Frogmore, near
Windsor, for the Prince
Consort, and she also
encouraged her subjects
to commemorate his
achievements with countless
public statues.

reported pit disasters, complete with artists' impressions of the explosions and collapsed tunnels. Artists also found ample scope for representing the wives of sailors, waiting for the good news that never came, set in the West Country, Scotland or Yorkshire.

Women of all classes also had to deal with the high rate of infant mortality. If their children survived beyond their first birthday, they still had to run the gauntlet of infections and accidents, as well as the epidemics of cholera and typhoid that were only tamed later in Victoria's reign. The images of dead or dying children that were tenderly displayed in novels, religious tracts and paintings were not mere sentiment. They reflected a very real fear of an early grave.

17. *The Fatal Accident at New Hartley Colliery: Removal of the Coffins. Illustrated London News* (1 February, 1862). V&A: PP 10.

The death rate declined a little during Victoria's reign, from 21.4 per 1,000 in the early 1840s to 17.7 per 1,000 in 1900, but some trades, notably mining and fishing, remained notoriously dangerous.

18. Mrs Alexander Farmer, *An Anxious Hour*. Oil on wood, 1865. V&A 541-1905.

In the mid-19th century, 15 per cent of children died before their first birthday, and many more struggled to survive the epidemics and accidents that beset them later in childhood.

CHILDREN AND ILLEGITIMACY

For the majority of married women, particularly until the emergence of new attitudes in the 1860s, it was only a matter of time before they became pregnant. During Victoria's reign there were several significant shifts in the way that women experienced pregnancy and childbirth. In the first case, the role of doctors became more formalised. The growing professionalisation of medicine meant that the traditional role of midwives was reduced. In addition, doctors were able to offer new methods of easing birth, and reducing pain. There were significant advances in the use of anaesthetics during the late 1840s, and in 1867 Joseph Lister developed an antiseptic spray, which also helped the medical profession. Until forceps and other obstetric equipment could be effectively sterilised, their use could significantly increase the risk of infection. Now, the most up-to-date doctors could intervene more effectively in difficult births.

There were, of course, several methods of avoiding the dangers of repeated pregnancy and childbirth. Breastfeeding, for example, reduced the likelihood of conception, and wealthier women, who were more inclined to give their infants to wet-nurses, could find it difficult to space their pregnancies as a result. Abortion was illegal, but that did not always deter shopkeepers from selling potions that were clearly labelled 'Not to be taken by expectant mothers'; they were sold on the understanding that they could induce a miscarriage. There are also accounts of back-street abortionists, such as the country 'dressmaker' who carried out abortions on two girls, Nelly and Sophy, before encouraging them to move to London,

19. Richard Redgrave, *The Outcast.* Oil on canvas, 1851. Royal Academy, London. The Poor Law Amendment Act of 1834 contained a 'bastardy' clause, which effectively punished women for immoral behaviour. The fathers of illegitimate children no longer had to take any responsibility for their upkeep, so unmarried mothers were forced into the workhouse.

widely used from the 1860s onwards, initially by the middle classes, and then by working families too. Annie Besant and Charles Bradlaugh drew attention to birth control when they published a booklet, *The Fruits of Philosophy*, in 1877, providing information on barrier methods, such as the pessary, sponge and condom, as

20 (left). Early inhaler for ether anaesthia. Glass, metal, sponge, wood and cloth, 1847–8. Science Museum, London / Science and Society Picture Library. The use of pain-relief during childbirth was popularised by the Queen, who testified to the effectiveness of

chloroform during the birth of her eighth child in 1853.

21 (below). Obstetrical forceps. Steel and ebony, *c.*1871–1900. Science Museum, London / Science and Society Picture Library.

where they became prostitutes. (We hear their story from one of their clients, 'Walter', who described his numerous sexual encounters in *My Secret Life*, a series of volumes that were printed in the 1890s for private circulation.)

Prostitutes and married women both benefited from the development of contraceptives during Victoria's reign, and by the end of the century it was clear that many couples were able to limit the size of their families. Despite some high-profile controversies, improved methods of contraception were becoming

well as promoting the use of the vaginal douche. They were both convicted of publishing 'an obscene libel', although their sentence of six months imprisonment was quashed on appeal. Although they were criticised for encouraging couples to enjoy sex for pleasure, rather than procreation, their advice was followed by an increasing number of women. During the last decades of Victoria's reign, contraceptives were more easily obtained and were widely marketed. They were advertised by travelling lecturers, in chemists' shops and in public conveniences. Mass-produced condoms, in the second half of the century, could cost as little as $^1/_2$ d each.

However many women still had to cope with the difficulties of an unwanted pregnancy. The stigma of illegitimacy did not lessen as the century progressed. As Thomas Hardy discovered in 1891, it was not appropriate for a family magazine such as *The Graphic* to publish a tale that referred explicitly to unmarried motherhood. In the first, serialised version of *Tess of the D'Urbervilles*, the brief existence of Tess's bastard child was left out of the story entirely.

In the public imagination, illegitimacy meant scandal and a downward spiral into vice. However, the Victorian perception of the careers of wayward women was not always borne out in reality. Despite the urgings of melodramatic heroines, few Victorian women felt it necessary to throw themselves off the nearest bridge to end their troubles. As we shall see, illicit sexuality was a fact of nineteenth-century life.

22. George Lawson, *Motherless*. Marble, *c.* 1889. Glasgow Museums: Kelvingrove.
Despite advances in medical care, death in childbirth was still a real fear for families.

PROSTITUTES AND MISTRESSES

Our preconceptions about Victorian sexuality are significantly undermined when we encounter such evidence of extra-marital sex. We are also likely to be surprised when we face up to the problems of co-habitation and prostitution in Victorian cities. In 1849 the journalist Henry Mayhew began to collect accounts for his social survey, *London Labour and the London Poor*, which provide an insight into both forms of illicit sexual behaviour. His interview with a costermonger lad, for example, made it clear that among the poorest classes, marriage, and indeed much formal morality, was irrelevant. Mayhew discovered that 'It is not at all uncommon for a lad of fifteen to be living with a girl of the same age, as man and wife. It creates no disgust among his class'.[10]

In other interviews he was told of the lax sexual relations between many young lodgers in the cheapest houses: 'Three, four, five, six and even more boys and girls have been packed head and feet, into one small bed ... there is an amicable interchange of partners, and next day a resumption of their former companionship.'[11] Mayhew's accounts suggested that it was a simple step from immodesty to prostitution. He also discovered that many women resorted to prostitution when seasonal work was slack; in the summer they could make a living as flower-girls or hop-pickers, but during the winter they would go back on the streets.

Recent studies of the time-lag between marriage and baptism of a first child have produced some startling results: up to one half of brides were pregnant when they reached the altar. This evidence for pre-nuptial conception comes from the parish registers of mid-Victorian England. Such information sheds new light on the problems of illegitimacy, as it seems that unmarried couples would often enjoy sexual relations in anticipation of marriage. In this scenario, many women who bore bastard children are likely to have expected to marry the father of their child, but for some reason the wedding never came about.

Such practices made it difficult for Victorian commentators to estimate the number of prostitutes working in London – suggestions varied wildly between 5,000 and 50,000 women. There were occasional outbursts of moral panic, when the

23 (opposite). Phoebus Levin, *The Dancing Platform at Cremorne Gardens* (detail). Oil on canvas, 1864. Museum of London. London's pleasure gardens provided the backdrop for much overt prostitution, as well as less clearly defined 'fast' behaviour.

24 (right). William Holman Hunt, *The Awakening Conscience*. Oil on canvas, 1853–4. Tate Gallery, London. Wealthy men would install their mistresses in the furnished apartments of St John's Wood, London. Hunt claimed that his painting of such a relationship was moral, as he chose to depict the moment when the kept woman decides to renounce her sinful life.

25. John Henry Henshall, *Behind the Bar* (detail). Oil on canvas, 1882. Museum of London.
According to one magazine of 1869, the life of a 'Refreshment-bar young lady' was 'a series of flirtations', but for many women it was the only way to make ends meet.

authorities tried to address the problem. Prostitutes were clearly visible in the pleasure gardens and parks of the capital. Courtesans displayed their elegantly-clad figures on horseback in Rotten Row, while lower-class women could be picked up in the Strand or Leicester Square.

It was this visibility that made prostitution such a contentious topic among Victorian commentators. It was a commonly-held belief, popularised in poems such as Thomas Hood's 'The Bridge of Sighs' (1844), that these women would soon succumb to disease and distress. However, William Acton, in his wide-ranging study *Prostitution considered in its Moral, Social and Sanitary Aspects* ... (1857), claimed that prostitutes were often healthier and more robust than women working in factories. This failed to reduce the fear of venereal disease. In an attempt to protect clients and, potentially, their chaste wives, the Contagious Diseases Acts were passed between 1864 and 1867. This legislation allowed the police to arrest any woman suspected of prostitution. She could then be forcibly examined for infection and, if thought necessary, hospitalised.

The Ladies' National Association was formed to demand the repeal of these Acts. It claimed that women were being categorised as either 'pure' or 'impure' and that their rights were being abused. It also attacked the implicit double standards of the Acts – the large numbers of men who resorted to prostitutes were not subjected to similar checks. The campaign was led by Josephine Butler (1828–1906), the daughter of a wealthy landowner. By her public speaking, she encouraged other respectable women to support the cause of those who had been driven to prostitution by poverty or circumstance.

Street prostitution was, of course, only the public face of Victorian sexual activity outside marriage. Other improper relationships included those carried out behind the curtains of London apartments, where wealthy men kept their mistresses. In less refined circles, artists' models, actresses and barmaids found themselves balanced precariously on the edge of respectable society. In fact, as Acton pointed out, the dividing line between innocence and vice was very difficult to define: 'prostitution is a transitory state, through which an untold number of British women are ever on their passage.'[12]

26. Dante Gabriel Rossetti,
Aurelia (Fazio's Mistress). Oil
on mahogany, 1863–73.
Tate Gallery, London.
Fanny Cornforth was working
as a prostitute when she
attracted Rossetti's attention
by pelting him with nut-
shells. She became one of
his favourite models, and
then his mistress and
'housekeeper'.

27. Giovanni Boldini,
*Gertrude Elizabeth Blood,
Lady Colin Campbell*. Oil on
canvas, *c*.1896. National
Portrait Gallery, London.
The accusations of adultery
made against Lady Colin
Campbell during her divorce
proceedings in 1886 caused
a sensation.

ART AND MORALITY

Victorian art critics stressed the depiction of the human body as a test of the artist's skill. Even if the figures were dressed in the finished picture, artists would often prepare nude studies first. As a result, artistic modelling was associated with impropriety. However, paintings and sculptures of nudes were acceptable if they idealised the female figure, and could be compared favourably with the smooth whiteness of classical sculpture. Artists were condemned if their nudes looked too realistic, as audiences did not want to be reminded of the working-class girls who were the models for nymphs and goddesses.

28. J. Watson, *Nude before a Mirror*. Photograph, *c.*1856. V&A: 36.373. Photographs that were nominally created to supplement life drawings made by artists soon began to slide into semi-pornography. Many were imported from France, where they were produced in industrial quantities.

29 (opposite). William Frost, *L'Allegro*. Oil painting, 1848. The Royal Collection © HM Queen Elizabeth II. Queen Victoria often shocked her artistic advisors by her cheerful enjoyment of nude subjects. She commissioned this painting as a gift for Prince Albert's birthday.

30. Sir John Everett Millais, *The Knight Errant*. Oil on canvas, 1870. Tate Gallery, London.
The female nude was made respectable by her affinity with Greek sculpture. Millais risked criticism for juxtaposing a naked model 'not over pure in character or refined in expression' with a sword-wielding, armour-clad knight. (F.G. Stephens, *Saturday Review*, 14 May 1870)

31 (left). John Gibson, *Tinted Venus*. Marble and paint, 1851–6. National Museums and Galleries on Merseyside. The whiteness of classical sculptures was an essential part of their purity. When Gibson coloured the skin and lips of his Venus, as the ancient Greeks would have done, he was accused of sensuality.

32 (right). Sir Lawrence Alma-Tadema, *The Sculptor's Model*. Oil on canvas, 1877. Private Collection.
The Victorian audience constantly struggled with the distinction between 'naked' and 'nude'. This overt comparison of a marble sculpture with its original working-class model caused 'An Offended Father' to write to the *Liverpool Mercury* on 13 September 1878, condemning 'such a painful and pernicious painting, its living model heartlessly purchased with gold, at the sacrifice of all feelings of delicacy'.

33. After Dante Gabriel Rossetti, *Maids of Elfenmere*. Engraving by the Dalziel Brothers, 1855. V&A: E.2923-1904.

Pre-Raphaelite artists delighted in exploring the sexual allure of women, and their pictures were often the forerunners of the *femmes fatale* of the 1890s.

34. Julia Margaret Cameron, *Merlin and Vivien*. Photograph album, 1874. V&A: 85-1970. Women who were aware of their own sexuality caused unease. Tennyson's poetry described how Vivien seduced Merlin, encouraged him to reveal the secret of his magic, and then used it against him.

35 (right). Sir Edward Burne-Jones, *The Tree of Forgiveness.* Oil on canvas, 1886. National Museums and Galleries on Merseyside.

The animal, primitive nature of women's sexual power was made explicit in the metamorphosing body of Phyllis. According to myth, she was transformed into an almond tree by grief at her lover's inconstancy.

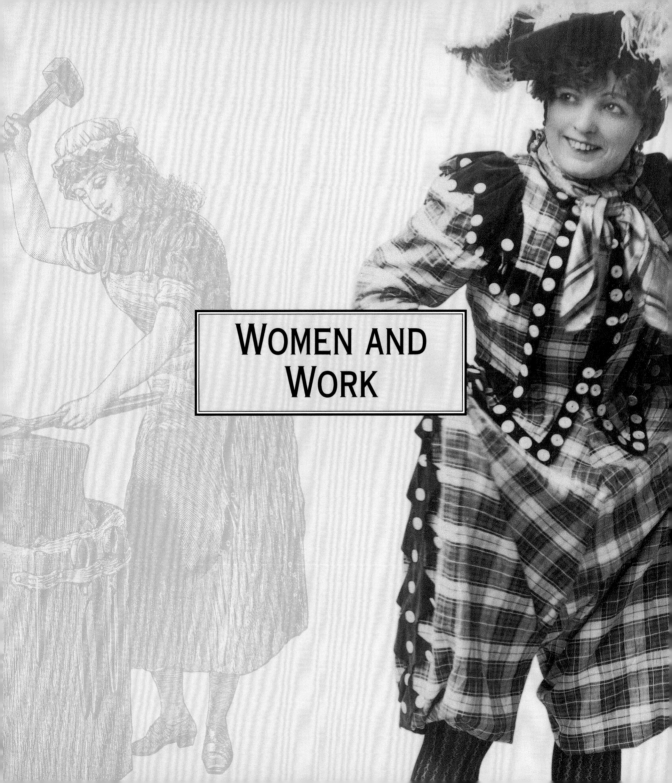

WOMEN AND WORK

SHOPPING

As part of her domestic duties, a woman was expected to make the home comfortable and herself attractive. As the century progressed, these homely responsibilities metamorphosed into a well-developed consumer culture. Isabella Beeton's guide to running a household was only the most famous contribution to a new genre in publishing. Magazines and books poured onto the market from the mid-century, providing advice for decorating the home, managing servants and offering hospitality. *The Lady's Treasury*, a journal edited by Mrs Warren from 1857, contained articles on literature and domestic economy, while other magazines were devoted to the latest Paris fashions.

Wealthy women who lived within range of the big cities were now being offered a huge choice of products and services. The rise of the department store, an import from the USA, made shopping a leisure activity as never before. The Army & Navy Stores first opened in 1871, were a treasure-trove for anyone contemplating an overseas trip,

36. *Advertisement for 'My Queen' Vel-Vel.* Published in *The Graphic*, 20 August 1887. V&A: PP.8.D. Advertisers took commercial advantage of the Queen's jubilees in 1887 and 1897.

while Liberty, founded in London in 1875, provided the fashionable hostess with Japanese and Indian ornaments. The introduction of electric lights and plate-glass windows towards the end of the century made Oxford Street and Regent Street a welcoming spectacle for the woman with money and time on her hands.

The development of the West End in London attracted other women. Poor but genteel girls could find employment as shop-assistants in the area's new, brightly-lit stores. A young lady who worked in a dress department would be 'engaged ... for certain qualifications of figure, in addition to educational acquirements. She must speak French (occasionally she understands German), and must, of course ... be quick at arithmetic, and possessed of winning address, even temper, and patience.'[13] With these qualifications, she could hope to save enough money to start a small business of her own, or, as was the case more often, to attract a respectable husband.

37. Paisley shawl, c.1849–5c
V&A: T.310-1928.
The growth of the Empire,
and Britain's power as a
trading nation, was reflectec
in women's costume. Indian
patterned shawls proved so
popular that they were soon
being copied by Scottish
manufacturers.

38. Dickinson, *Indian Court
at the Great Exhibition*, 1851.
Colour lithograph, 1854.
V&A: 19536:11.
Women were well-
represented among the
visitors to the Crystal Palace,
the new South Kensington
museums and the annual
Royal Academy exhibitions.

DOMESTIC SERVICE AND MANUAL LABOUR

39. Thomas Woolner, *The Housemaid*. Bronze, 1890s. Salter's Company.
Domestic servants made up the largest group of working women, and outnumbered men by nine to one. In 1851, over 900,000 women were in service, rising to 1.3 million in 1871.

40. James Tissot, *Too Early* (detail). Oil on canvas, 1873. Guildhall Art Gallery.
Housemaids, cooks and laundry-women were essential adjuncts to the rise of the Victorian middle and upper classes. A wife could only maintain her respectable status if she was supported by a number of working women.

42 (below). *Hop-picking*. Plate from *Illustrated London News*, 2 Oct 1858. V&A: PP.10. Families from London and itinerant labourers took advantage of seasonal work in the hop-gardens of Kent. There were only about 220,000 women working full-time on farms in 1851, and their numbers fell by a further 40 per cent over the next 20 years. Working as a field labourer was more arduous than domestic service, and most agricultural jobs were taken by men.

41 (above). *Women Surface Workers, Lancashire*. Photograph, mid 19th century. National Coalmining Museum Collection.
In 1842 women were forbidden from working underground in the mining industry. Some pockets of employment remained, including the bal-maidens, who sorted the tin-ore in the West Country, and the pit-head lasses of Lancashire.

43 (right). David Octavius Hill and Robert Adamson, *Oyster Woman*. Photograph, 1850s. V&A: 67.3888.
The nature of women's work was largely regional. In fishing communities their jobs would include preparing and selling the catch.

SEAMSTRESSES AND MILLINERS

44. John Thomson, *An Old Clothes' Shop, Seven Dials*. Photograph, 1876–7. V&A: PH.992-1978.
Henry Mayhew noted how women minding the clothes' shops around Petticoat Lane 'sit in the street carrying on their domestic occupations ... shelling peas ... trimming vegetables ... plying their needles.'

45 (opposite). Tenniel, *The Ghost in the Looking Glass*. Plate from *Punch*, 4 July 1863. V&A: PP.8.J.
Thomas Hood's poem 'The Song of the Shirt' (1843) raised awareness of the distress suffered by seamstresses: 'A woman sat, in unwomanly rags ... In poverty, hunger and dirt ... Sewing at once, with a double thread, A shroud as well as a shirt.'

46. Prof. Henry Tonks, *The Hat Shop*. Oil on canvas, 1892. Birmingham City Museum and Art Gallery. Young women from lower middle-class families could work in the relative gentility of a milliner's.

Needlework was also considered to be an appropriate occupation for a woman. As a necessary domestic skill for women of all classes, it was a supposedly genteel way for poverty-stricken girls to make a living. However, the reality of life as a seamstress was often shockingly hard. A girl could either take on piecework in her own home or live under the roof of her employer. In both of these scenarios, she was expected to pay for her own thread, buttons, candles and heating, all of which ate into her meagre earnings.

Novelists, poets and painters drew attention to the plight of such women. Charles Dickens was particularly scathing of the conditions in which young seamstresses were set to work. He criticised the 'dulness, unhealthy confinement and bodily fatigue' that was suffered by Kate Nickleby when she worked as a dressmaker for Madame Mantalini.[14]

Several commentators professed themselves to be unsurprised that women would prefer prostitution to this tedious poverty. Their situation was marginally improved by the introduction of the sewing machine, an American import, in the second half of Victoria's reign, but, even at the end of the nineteenth century, women made up the bulk of employees in the sweated industries.

PUNCH, OR THE LONDON CHARIVARI—July 4, 1863.

THE HAUNTED LADY, OR "THE GHOST" IN THE LOOKING-GLASS.
Madame La Modiste. "WE WOULD NOT HAVE DISAPPOINTED YOUR LADYSHIP, AT ANY SACRIFICE, AND THE ROBE IS FINISHED *J MERVEILLE*"

FACTORIES AND WORKSHOPS

47. *Manufacturing pens, Birmingham, pen grinding room, and slitting room.* Plate from *Illustrated London News*, 22 February 1851. V&A: PP..10.

Women were employed in many of the metal workshops that sprang up in and around Birmingham.

There were forceful reasons behind women's choice to work at home, making shirts, paper bags, or toys, despite the poor wages that they received. It made childcare easier, and fitted in more closely with the ideal of female domesticity. Women who went out to work in factories and workshops were chided for their poor housekeeping and their unfeminine independence. Critics condemned the factory hand as 'the most unthrifty, ignorant, slovenly housekeeper in the world'.[15] Of course, this reproof took no account of the fact that all working mothers were effectively doing a 'double-shift' each day: labouring in the factory from dawn to dusk, and then at home, where they would still be expected to bake bread for the family, do their washing and clean the house.

For many women in the industrial cities, working in the local textile mill was the only way to make ends meet. By 1900, nearly a quarter of a million women were employed in the cotton mills of Lancashire alone. As soon as they could pass the 'Labour Exam', children began working in the mills in the morning and going to school in the afternoon; at 14 they were expected to work full-time. A young girl could add 7 shillings a week to the family income, but even grown women found it hard to bring home more than 12 shillings, even at the end of the century. The majority of factory girls gave up work when they married, and their notorious independence soon evaporated once they had a family to keep.

The employment of women in the textile mills drew unprecedented attention from commentators, who raised fears about child welfare and the boldness of factory hands. Other industries that employed large numbers of women attracted less comment. In the Black Country, for instance, many women could be found in the metal trades, sometimes working alongside men. The Potteries of North Staffordshire made a virtue of feminine neatness, by employing women to decorate ceramics. In fact, many of these industries stressed that women were especially suited to such dextrous work. They were also, inevitably, cheaper to hire and, despite their lower wages, were categorised as more reliable and less likely to agitate for better pay and conditions. Thus the female characteristics of docility and delicacy, which usually implied the need for protection within the domestic sphere, were instead used to justify the employment of women in large-scale industry.

48. Eyre Crowe, *The Dinner Hour, Wigan*. Oil on canvas, 1874. Manchester City Art Gallery.

Factory girls could begin working full-time at 14, adding 7 shillings a week to the family income.

ENTERTAINMENT

49 (left). James Tissot, *Hush – the Concert*. Oil on canvas, *c*.1875. Manchester City Art Galleries.
Professional virtuosi were in demand for private parties and public concerts. But the musical skills that were nurtured in young ladies were redefined once they were used to earn a living.

50 (right). *Marie Lloyd*. Photograph, *c*.1890. V&A: Theatre Museum.
Working-class entertainers could find a ready audience in music-halls. The disreputable 'penny-gaffs' described by Mayhew in 1850, had been transformed by the end of the century into lavishly decorated, respectable venues.

51 (left). John Singer Sargent, *Ellen Terry as Lady Macbeth*. Oil on canvas, 1889. Tate Gallery, London. Talented actresses such as Ellen Terry and Mrs Patrick Campbell became well-known public figures, welcomed in polite society. However, women who had been on the stage always retained a hint of impropriety.

52 (opposite). *Lulu As She Appeared Before Their Royal Highnesses The Prince and Princess of Wales.* Playbill, 1871. V&A: Theatre Museum. In the 1840s there had been a vogue for *tableaux vivants*, in which mythological scenes were acted out by girls wearing tight-fitting 'fleshings'. During the 1860s and '70s, these entertainments were eclipsed by sensational, scantily-clad acrobats. Social commentators often found it hard to draw a distinction between these acts and overt prostitution.

LuLu

ROYAL HIGH AMPHITHEATRE. HOLBORN.

EVERY EVENING, & WEDNESDAY & SATURDAY AFTERNOON.

EVERY EVENING, & WEDNESDAY & SATURDAY AFTERNOON.

STANNARD & SON, 7, POLAND ST LONDON. W.

AS SHE APPEARED BEFORE THEIR ROYAL HIGHNESSES, THE PRINCE & PRINCESS OF WALES, FEB.Y 20.TH 1871.

ART AND LITERATURE

Poets, novelists and painters could also be criticised for deliberately seeking public approbation. Christina Rossetti was not alone in believing that publishing her poems would seem conceited, and she struggled with her desire to write and be recognised. Some women got around this problem by using male pseudonyms: Charlotte Brontë, for example, wrote as Currer Bell. As the century progressed, attitudes towards women writers became more liberal. This was partly the result of new opportunities for publishing. With the boom in books and magazines devoted to interior decoration, fashion and housekeeping, women were able to launch themselves into journalism.

Painters and sculptors also benefited from changes in exhibitions and art education during the second half of the century. Nearly one quarter of the artists invited to exhibit at the Grosvenor Gallery in 1877 were women. A large number of female artists also showed their work at the annual Royal Academy

53 (below). Lady Elizabeth Butler, *The Roll Call*. Oil on canvas, 1874. The Royal Collection © HM Queen Elizabeth II.
This young artist gained immediate fame at her first Royal Academy exhibition, when the Queen bought her picture of the Crimean War.

54 (opposite). Paul Chapuis, *Woman painting portrait*. Handcoloured stereoscopic photograph, c.1860. V&A: E.1209-1992.
Young ladies were expected to be able to paint a little, but their work was rarely taken seriously.

exhibitions. Here they were at more of a disadvantage, as all the Hanging Committee were men and, until 1860, women could not study at the Royal Academy schools.

Many women made successful careers as artists, despite these handicaps. Often they took to painting because it was the family business, and they learned the trade alongside their brothers. Rebecca Solomon, for example, followed her two brothers, Abraham and Simeon, into the studio, and became a successful painter in her own right, and Evelyn De Morgan picked up her distinctive style from her uncle, Spencer Stanhope. Frequently, however, women would be encouraged to focus on feminine subjects, such as domestic scenes, still lifes and flower pieces, rather than tackle history, myth or *plein air* landscapes. Even among professional women, a sense of respectability could be retained by allusion to the accomplishments of amateur young ladies.

During Victoria's reign, many women painters and writers began to challenge the accepted parameters of female activity. By using traditional accomplishments as a starting point, they escaped from the confines of the domestic sphere.

55. Frederic Hollyer, *Mary Watts, Wife of G.F. Watts*. Photograph, late 19th century. V&A: 7810-1938. The Arts and Crafts movement encouraged young ladies to use their skills in embroidery, enamelling and pottery. Mary Watts designed and helped to build a memorial chapel for her husband near Guildford at the turn of the 20th century.

56. *The Slade Life-Class.*
Plate from *Magazine of Art*,
vol. 6, 1883. V&A: PP.400.S.
Until 1860, women could not
study in the official Royal
Academy schools. Even after
Laura Herford gained a
place, using only her initials
on her application, access to
life-classes was forbidden
until 1893, so many women
chose to attend classes at
the Slade instead.

PIONEERING WOMEN

NEW OPPORTUNITIES AT WORK

57 (above). *The Telephone Exchange in London*. Plate from the *Graphic* (September 1883). V&A: PP.8.D-E. Women were felt to be especially suited to the new jobs of telegraph 'manipulator' and telephone operator. From the invention of the telegraph in 1837, girls with nimble fingers, patience and a polite manner were in great demand. Their new-found independence would be short-lived, as most employers would expect a woman to leave her job as soon as she married.

58 (right). Lucien Faure, *Empire Typewriter*. Poster, 1897. V&A: Circ. 586-1962 The invention of the typewriter enabled more middle-class women to enter the workplace. From the 1880s, with a typing course under their belt, they could find carefully supervised work in local government offices or commercial organisations, where they were usually segregated from male employees.

THE 'GIRL OF THE PERIOD'

Some young women found shocking ways of breaking the boundaries of their protected upbringing. During the 1860s, some independently-minded wealthy girls caused a sensation by emulating the fashions and behaviour of courtesans. These 'Girls of the Period' were the subject of outraged newspaper articles, criticising their 'false red hair and painted skin, talking slang as glibly as a man, and by preference leading the conversations to doubtful subjects. She thinks she is piquant and exciting when she thus makes herself the bad copy of a worst original; and she will not see that though men laugh with her they do not respect her; though they flirt with her, they do not marry her.'[16] They repeatedly advised 'that no good girl can afford to appear bad' for fear of being treated like one of the demi-monde.[17]

The number of young ladies of good families who actually took to drinking, smoking and going about town in search of amusement was in reality rather small, but certainly journalists were responding to a change in attitude. Until the late 1860s, respectable women tried to slip unobserved through London's streets, and were commonly chaperoned. The city centre was male dominated, and women in the streets did not want to be mistaken for prostitutes. From the 1870s, however, London and the other large cities offered wealthy unmarried girls new opportunities for shopping, visiting art galleries and eating out, while the less well off could take up clerical jobs in town. As a result, women were more commonly seen using public transport for their daily journeys to and from work.

So perhaps it would be more sensible to look upon the 'Girl of the Period' as an exaggerated version of the many young women who, in the 1860s and 1870s, began to emerge from the domestic sphere. A change in attitude was being brought about, not by the actions of a radical few, but by the quiet determination of the many middle-class women who passed through the city every day, for work and pleasure.

59 (opposite). William Maw Egley, *Omnibus Life in London.* Oil on canvas, 1859. Tate Gallery, London. Buses and trams allowed women more freedom to negotiate the city streets.

THE 'NEW WOMAN'

Some 30 years after the emergence of the 'Girl of the Period' there was another flurry of criticism about the unconventional behaviour of young ladies. Journalists in the 1890s began to discuss the phenomenon of the 'New Woman'. She had much in common with her 1860s forebear: she smoked, entered boldly into conversation with men and was seen around town (although now she was on a bicycle). She had also acquired certain distinctive characteristics. The flirtations of the 'Girl of the Period' were replaced by an unfeminine disdain for marriage. The New Woman's independence was enhanced by her work, as she was frequently imagined as a controversial writer or artist, or engaged in political campaigning. Her intellectual capacity made her an object of disgust to many commentators. While the girls of the 1860s had caused a stir because of their overt sensuality, the New Woman was more likely to be presented as unattractive and masculine.

Like the satires of the 1860s, in many cases the New Woman was an exaggeration of more subtle changes in the position of young women. She reflected establishment fears of the new legal status of women who could control their own finances, attend university and come and go as they pleased. By the end of the century, both in fact and in fiction, many more women were willing to live without the safety net of male support.

60 (left). Aubrey Beardsley, *The Idler: Advanced Woman Number*. Magazine cover, 1894. V&A: E.3025-1921. In 1893, George Egerton, the female author of *Keynotes*, described the New Woman's 'restless craving for sun and love and motion' and her 'frank and unembarrassed gaze'.

61 (opposite). Alfred Morrow, *The New Woman*. Theatre poster, 1894. V&A: E.2682-1962. Sydney Grundy's play, which opened in September 1894, satirised the 'unfeminine' aspects of intellectual women.

SPORT

62 (left). *National Archery Meeting, Exeter*. Plate from *Illustrated London News*, 7 August 1858. V&A: PP.10. In the 1850s, girls were encouraged to try their hands at archery, and in the next decade there was a craze for croquet.

63 (right). Paul Martin, *Girls Paddling at Cromer*. Photograph, 1892. V&A:1728-1980. Queen Victoria had set a trend for sea bathing when she first visited the Isle of Wight in the 1840s. By the end of the century, many women were able to enjoy a day out at the seaside, thanks to the introduction of special excursion fares on the railways.

64 (right). Photograph of three women on bicycles, from a family photograph album. Platinum print, 1898. V&A: E.2283-1997.
During the 1880s and '90s young women were able to learn to cycle, and were criticised by Eliza Lynn Linton for enjoying 'the intoxication that comes from unfettered liberty'. Diffident girls pedalled around on tricycles that accommodated their skirts, but more daring friends sat astride their bicycles.

65 (opposite). *Mrs Bloomer's Own.* Song sheet, 1850s. V&A: Enthoven Collection.
Physical exertion was hampered by bulky skirts and unwieldy hats. The American, Mrs Bloomer caused a sensation by introducing knickerbockers to Britain in the 1850s. They were ideal for cycling, but were severely criticised for their masculine appearance.

66 (overleaf). Sir John Lavery, *The Tennis Party*. Oil on canvas, 1886. Aberdeen Art Gallery.
Towards the end of the 19th century, women participated in far more active sports. Leisurely games of tennis were an ideal way to meet young men, and more determined women could play at the Wimbledon Championships from 1884.

DRESS

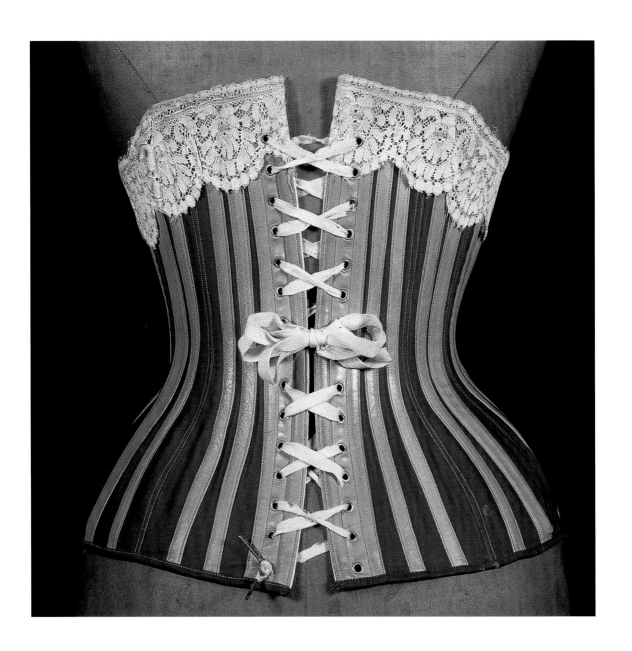

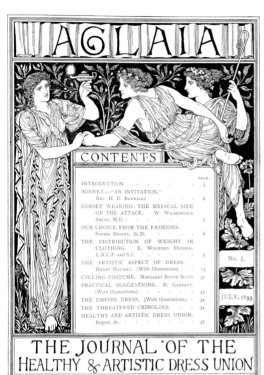

THE JOURNAL OF THE HEALTHY & ARTISTIC DRESS UNION

67 (left). Red satin corset with yellow leather. 1884. V&A: T.84-1980. Complex undergarments were considered essential in order to support the weaker female body.

68 (above). *Aglaia*. Magazine cover, 1893. V&A: PP.4.N. In some artistic circles, 'rational' dress became fashionable. It was originally associated with Pre-Raphaelite artists whose models were draped in drooping velvet and muslin.

69 (right). Crinoline spring steel hoop frame, cotton chemise, whalebone corset. *c.*1860–9. V&A: 86-1935. The fashionable silhouette changed dramatically during Victoria's reign, from whalebone or steel-framed crinoline, to the padded or cantilevered bustle.

INTREPID WOMEN

70. Dillwyn Llewelyn Jones, *Caswell Bay*. Photograph, 1853. V&A: PH.165-1984. Natural history and geology became favourite topics of study after Darwin sparked evolutionary debates with his publication of *The Origin of Species* in 1859.

Even at the farthest outposts of the Empire, many Victorian women felt it was only proper to retain their conventional dress. Mary Kingsley (1862–1900) firmly declared that 'you have no right to go about Africa in things you would be ashamed to be seen in at home.' Occasionally her stiff black silk dress could be a positive life-saver. On one expedition she found herself 'in a heap, on a lot of spikes ... at the bottom of a ... game pit. It is at these times you realise the blessing of a good thick skirt'.[18] She had come to West Africa in 1893, after the death of her parents, to collect fish and to gain an understanding of African cultures. She was not alone in her desire for independent travel, but, like many women, she found that she could only do so when she was freed from her domestic responsibilities.

71. Felice Beato, *Climbing the Pyramids*. Photograph, *c.* 1870. V&A: X 831.46. Victorian women rarely seem to have been daunted by the opportunities which came their way during their overseas tours.

Overseas travel gave women a chance to exert themselves in ways that would have seemed inappropriate at home. Lady Anne Blunt, for example, travelled extensively with her husband in the Arabian desert. Despite the trials of sleeping in rough tents, fighting off hostile horsemen and her own ill-health, she found a peace that she could never experience with her philandering husband at home. She published an account of their wanderings in *The Bedouin Tribes of the Euphrates* in 1879.

Unlike these wealthy women, who travelled by choice, many Victorians were compelled by circumstance to undertake long and arduous journeys. Some families decided that emigration was preferable to life in the industrial cities of Britain, and set off for the gold fields of Australia, or the prairies

72 (opposite). Marianne North, *Flowers of Datura and Hummingbird, Brazil.* Oil on canvas, 1870s. Kew Gardens, Richmond.

Marianne North travelled extensively, from Chile to Sarawak, capturing the intense colours of flowers and landscapes in her paintings. A gallery devoted to her work was opened at Kew Gardens in 1882.

73 (right). *Grotte du glacier des Bossons.* Photograph, 1889. V&A: PH.1161-1908.

Stout-hearted women armed themselves with staves and shortened skirts to ascend the Alps: 'a whole army of distant peaks begins to start into sight: and so, after six hours, we all at once find ourselves upon the top!' (Amelia Edwards, 1873)

of North America. Conditions here were tough, and women received little advice on coping with their new situation. *The A.B.C. of Colonisation* suggested that 'The great art of bush-cookery consists in giving a variety out of salt beef and flour, minus mustard, pepper and potatoes ... Every woman who values her husband's health will give him a hot meal every day.'[19] It went on to provide ideas for seven different dishes to be made from these limited ingredients.

Nothing could prepare emigrants for the extreme climates they had to face. Lady Barker's household in New Zealand suffered in the bitter winters. She described the desperation when they found that 'there was now not a particle of food in the house. The servants remained in their beds, declining to get up, and alleging that they might as well "die warm".'[20] This family survived the ordeal, but many others around the Empire were far less fortunate as they struggled to contend with considerably more than a hostile climate.

The sufferings of British women during the Mutiny of the Indian army in 1857 became legendary. On 10 May, Kate Moore, sister of the postmaster of Meerut, sent a telegraph to Agra, warning that local Indian soldiers had killed their British officers. The uprising soon spread, and British families had to flee for their lives. Madeline Jackson, aged 17, was staying with relatives in Sitapur, when she was forced to escape from the house: 'Directly we were out, we ran across an open plain, towards the jungles, thinking my sister was with us. Then I noticed an extraordinary whistling noise everywhere and stopped: I had never been out like that ... in the middle of the day before and

thought it had something to do with the sun! [I] said "what's that?" My brother quietly answered "the bullets."' Later she was able to describe her ordeal as they trekked through rivers and jungle, and heard tales of slaughter from a group of Parsees who stopped to help them: 'they told us Mr and Mrs Christian and the baby were killed: he was shot, she sat down by him crying and they went and cut off her head, and the poor baby they took up on a spear and threw into the river.'[21] Such atrocities were widely reported back in Britain, and contributed to a growing sense of outrage at the actions of the mutineers. The British army responded to this treatment of the memsahibs with swift and dreadful punishments. However, some women found that, paradoxically, the Mutiny gave them a chance to confront their conventional passive roles. One survivor explained 'Some men may think that women are weak, and only fitted to do trivial things, and endure petty troubles ... but there are many who can endure with fortitude and patience what even soldiers shrink from. Men are fitted by education and constitution to dare to do; yet they have been surpassed, in presence of mind, and power of endurance, by weak women.'[22]

Many Victorian women discovered that the ideal female of the British drawing-room could rise to the challenges of foreign experience, and discover within herself the resilience and independence to survive.

74. Abraham Solomon, *The Flight from Lucknow*. Oil on canvas, 1858. Leicester Museums and Art Gallery.
Some 2,000 people, including 400 European women and children, were besieged in Lucknow from 30 May to 16 November 1857 during the Indian Mutiny.

WOMEN AND EDUCATION

75 (opposite). Elizabeth Stanhope Forbes, *School is Out.* Oil on canvas, 1889. Penzance Town Council.
From 1870, the Elementary Education Act helped to fund local board schools, providing jobs for middle-class women and access to education for working-class children. School attendance was not compulsory until 1880, however, and even then, any child over 10 years old could work part-time.

76 (right). Richard Redgrave, *The Governess.* Oil on canvas, 1844. V&A: FA. 168
In wealthier families, a girl's education depended on the quality of her governess. Her tuition would often focus on the domestic skills of needlework, drawing and music-making, in addition to some French, history and geography. The life of a governess, although respectable, was regarded as arduous and lonely: 'Governess indeed! ... play the piano after dinner and day's work, be snubbed by the family, sneered at by the servants, and leered at by the young fellows! All for twenty pounds a year'. (*Girl of the Period Miscellany*, 1869)

77 (bottom right). *Graduates of Royal Holloway College.* Photograph, 1893. Royal Holloway and Bedford New College.
Until women could enter university, or one of the professions, there was little

incentive to advanced study. In 1847, Queen's College for Women opened, followed in 1849 by Bedford College and Royal Holloway College in 1886. Women received some recognition in the ancient universities by the establishment of Newnham (1871) and Girton (1872) colleges in Cambridge, but they were not admitted to full degrees.

WOMEN AND MEDICINE

78 (left). Jerry Barrett, *Mission of Mercy – Florence Nightingale Receiving the Wounded at Scutari*. Oil on canvas, 1856–8. National Portrait Gallery, London.
In 1854, Nightingale left her position as superintendent of a sanatorium to lead a team of nurses to the Crimea. At Scutari she found the wards filthy, and soldiers dying, not of wounds, but of infection. By the time she returned home, having reformed the military hospitals, she was a national heroine. The value of professional nurses was recognised for the first time in 1860, when St Thomas's Hospital, London, opened its training school for nurses.

79 (below). Illustration of Elizabeth Garrett (later Anderson) passing her doctoral examination at the Faculté de Medicine, Paris. From *Le Monde illustre* (25 June 1870). Mary Evans Picture Library.
Although women were expected to tend the sick, they were unable to qualify as doctors or surgeons. In 1860, Elizabeth Garrett began to attend medical lectures for trainee doctors at the Middlesex Hospital, but was denied access when a male student complained. The Society of Apothecaries changed their regulations to stop further women from taking their exams after she entered the profession by this route in 1865. In 1866 she established a dispensary for women in London, and in 1872, opened a hospital staffed entirely by women. She joined forces with Sophia Jex-Blake, who studied medicine at Edinburgh, to found the London Medical School for Women. Their persistence was rewarded in 1876 when an Act of Parliament forced medical schools to accept women on equal terms with men.

WOMEN'S MISSION

Throughout the nineteenth century, a woman's mission was broadly defined as providing emotional support for her family. Occasionally this sympathetic role could be expanded to appeal for change in a broader sphere. At the start of the century, for example, women used their moral position to agitate for the abolition of slavery. This part of their mission succeeded in 1833, when slavery was banned in British territories.

During Victoria's reign, women's philanthropic focus changed, becoming 'women's mission to women'. They turned their attention to the problems of poverty and prostitution that were all too visible in the industrial centres. Josephine Butler was voluble in her attempts to improve the lot of the 'Fallen Woman', but many other women worked in more modest ways. In the 1850s and 1860s, many streetwalkers were invited to 'midnight meetings' where they were offered refuge in Penitentiaries. These Magdalen Homes were supposed to be havens of mercy, not judgement, and many were staffed by young ladies who were undeterred by the controversial nature of their voluntary work. The prospectus for one such home indicated the

80 (opposite). *Fancy fair at the Pavilion, for the benefit of the Brighton Dispensary.* Plate from *Illustrated London News,* 22 March 1851.
V&A: PP 10.
Fundraising fairs were a sociable way of supporting charities.

81 (right). Ford Madox Brown, *Work* (detail). Oil on canvas, 1852–65. Manchester City Art Gallery.
In Brown's allegory of moral and immoral occupations, a well-dressed young lady carries pamphlets in support of the temperance movement.

82. *Dressing the Church with Holly*. Plate from *Illustrated London News*, 18 December 1869. V&A: PP 10.
Parish work, whether visiting the sick or decorating the church for festivals, was an appropriate use of a young ladies' time.

motivation for these volunteers. It 'earnestly hoped that ladies who act as Sisters will be led by God's grace to join this work'.[23]

Certainly, many women were encouraged in their mission by religious belief. Their involvement in the life of the parish church was an extension of the duties of the domestic sphere. With the rise of the High Church movement, women were able to participate in new ways. Journalists were often scathing about the ladies who flocked to an eager young curate and encouraged 'the aesthetic and sensual gratification which springs from Church services conducted with swinging lamps, with gorgeous vestments, with incense, with much posturing and intoning.'[24] These criticisms failed to take into account that the curate required the help of female parishioners in decorating the church with flowers, embroidering the richly-coloured vestments and cleaning brass candlesticks. Skills that had been developed as domestic duties now became significant as part of a wider theological debate. As in other cases, women's work could be adapted to allow them considerable influence in the changes that troubled Victorian society.

WOMEN AND POLITICS

83. *The Preston Strike – Mr Cowell addressing an open air meeting.* Plate from *Illustrated London News*, 12 November 1853. V&A: PP.10. Women were enthusiastic supporters of the trade union movement, from its earliest days.

In spite of their improved status by the end of Victoria's reign, women still could not exercise full political power. Although female ratepayers could nominally vote in local elections from 1869, and for parochial councils from 1894, they would not be eligible to vote in Parliamentary elections until 1918.

Politics were not the first concern for many working women: improved pay and conditions were more important than the vote. In 1891, for example, the mill-girl Selina Cooper led her colleagues in a trade union dispute to demand decent toilet facilities in her cotton factory. At the same time she asked the union to consider her objections to the sexual harassment of the mill-hands. This case illustrates the increasing overlap between trade union campaigners and the female suffrage movement. Undeterred by her limited success in 1891, Cooper went on to join the recently founded Independent Labour Party, and became involved in the campaign for women's votes.

The case of the Match-Girls' Strike provides another example of the close relationship between trade unions and female suffrage. In 1888, Annie Besant, a wealthy advocate of birth-control and supporter of female suffrage, turned her attention to the plight of young women in the Bryant & May match factory. These girls were being disfigured by the dangerous phosphorus fumes in the factory, and their low wages were often further reduced by fines. She helped the workers to form a Match-Girls' Union, and after a three-week strike, both their pay and conditions were improved.

Annie Besant's motivation came from an alternative, middle-class intellectual tradition. In these circles, the call for women's suffrage was encouraged by John Stuart Mill's book *Subjection of Women* (1869). When Mill gained a seat in Parliament, the radical Ladies' Discussion Society, founded in Kensington by Dorothea Beale, Elizabeth Garrett Anderson, Barbara Bodichon and others, decided to pursue this advantage. They organised a petition, containing around 1,500 signatures, asking Parliament to grant women the vote. The petition was unsuccessful, and Mill's attempt to extend women's voting rights in the 1867 Reform Act was defeated by 196 votes to 73.

Trade unions and the intellectual tradition of John Stuart Mill provided two routes to suffragist support. Another was socialism. Regional suffrage societies were established in Manchester, London, Edinburgh and Bristol, and many women were drawn into suffrage debates via the growing socialist movement. Some women were attracted into the political arena by the Clarion Cycling Clubs, first established in 1894. Their Sunday outings combined exercise and enjoyment with opportunities for publicising both the socialist and the suffrage message.

Although radical suffragette activity was an Edwardian invention, it is clear that there were small groups of Victorian women, both high- and low-born, who were agitating for political change. In doing this, they were bound to be controversial. Unlike other areas of activity, such as medicine, education or philanthropy, they could not argue that they were simply extending their domestic virtues into a slightly wider sphere.

The female suffrage campaign was severely criticised, not least by other women. The Queen was particularly horrified by the notion. Throughout her long reign she maintained her belief that women should hold sway in their own domain – the home – and leave men to deal with public matters. Her own position as Queen and Empress did not change her opinion. She accepted the duties that came with her inherited position, but she relied on her ministers, and on her husband, for support. Her family was her primary focus, and the doctrine of separate spheres appealed to her. Her life celebrated the centrality of Christian faith, self-discipline and patriotism.

84. *Convicts and Lunatics Have No Vote For Parliament.* Poster, c.1900. Mary Evans Picture Library / Fawcett Library.

The founding of the National Union of Women's Suffrage Societies in 1897 heralded a new era in the campaign for women's rights.

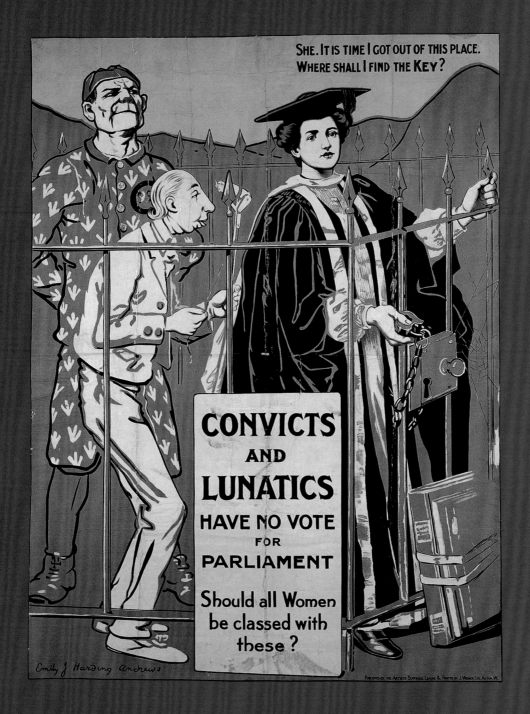

AFTERWORD

The experiences of Victorian women were infinitely varied, and their responses cannot be categorised easily. The broad range of activities in which they were involved breaks down the monolithic image of the idealised woman.

Stereotypes such as 'The Angel in the House' and the 'New Woman' represented an attempt to create a framework for acceptable behaviour, at a time when society was shifting beneath the feet of the Victorians.

The phenomenal growth in the urban population and technological developments that encouraged women to go out to work caused disruption in settled families. Novelists, journalists, artists, politicians and many housewives were all trying to deal with this frightening fluidity. Their attempt to limit the role of women was just one part of the much larger Victorian obsession with respectability, and what defined it. The answer would constantly elude them.

NOTES ON THE TEXT

1. Woolf, Virginia. *The Death of the Moth* (1942), quoted by Anstruther (1992), p.2.

2. 'The Girl of the Period', reprinted verbatim from the *Saturday Review* (Bristol and London, 1868), p.3.

3. Acton, William. *The Functions and Disorders of the Reproductive Organs* (1st edition 1857), quoted by Mason (1994), p.195.

4. Anonymous quotation, in Mason (1994), p.200.

5. Quoted by Mason (1994), p.203.

6. Publication by the Female Political Union of Newcastle-upon-Tyne (1839), quoted by Kingsley Kent (1999), p.171.

7. Disraeli, Benjamin. *Sybil* (1995), p.84.

8. Quoted by Kingsley Kent (1999), p.184.

9. Quoted by H.R.H. the Duchess of York (1991), p.164.

10. Mayhew (1965), p.12.

11. Mayhew (1965), p.60.

12. Quoted by Marcus (1970), p.6.

13. *The Girl of the Period Miscellany* (London, 1869), p.44.

14. Dickens, Charles. *Nicholas Nickleby* (1838–9).

15. *The Girl of the Period Miscellany* (London, 1869), p.186.

16. 'The Girl of the Period', reprinted verbatim from the *Saturday Review* (Bristol and London, 1868), p.10.

17. 'The Girl of the Period', reprinted verbatim from the *Saturday Review* (Bristol and London, 1868), p.6

18. Kingsley, Mary. *Travels in West Africa* (1897), quoted by Robinson (1994), pp.189, 214. Mary Kingsley is thought to have embellished tales of her African adventures for dramatic effect.

19. Chisolm, Caroline. *The A.B.C. of Colonization* (1850), quoted by Robinson (1994), p.345.

20. Barker, Lady. *Station Life in New Zealand* (1870), quoted by Robinson (1994), p.360.

21. Robinson (1996), pp.64, 65.

22. Coopland, Ruth. *A Lady's Escape from Gwalior* (1859), quoted by Robinson (1996), p.253.

23. Quoted by Marsh (1994), p.219.

24. 'The Ritualistic Girl', *The Girl of the Period Miscellany* (London, 1869), p.63.

SELECT BIBLIOGRAPHY

Ian Anstruther, *Coventry Patmore's Angel: A study of Coventry Patmore, his wife Emily, and The Angel in the House* (Haggerston Press, London, 1992)

ed. Susan P. Casteras and Colleen Denney, *The Grosvenor Gallery: A Palace of Art in Victorian England* (Yale University Press, New Haven and London, 1996

Wilkie Collins, *The Woman in White* (this ed: Oxford University Press, Oxford, 1996)

Chris Cook, *The Longman Companion to Britain in the Nineteenth Century 1815-1914* (Longman, London and New York, 1999)

Charles Dickens, *Hard Times* (this ed: Penguin Books, London, 1994)

Charles Dickens, *Our Mutual Friend* (this ed: Oxford University Press, Oxford, 1998)

Benjamin Disraeli, *Sybil* (this ed: Wordsworth Editions, Hertfordshire, 1995)

George Egerton, *Keynotes* (Elkin Mathews and John Lane, Boston, 1893)

George Eliot, *The Mill on the Floss* (this ed: Penguin Books, London, 1994)

Eric J. Evans, *The Forging of the Modern State: Early Industrial Britain 1783-1870* (Longman, London and New York, 1996)

Thomas Hardy, *Tess of the D'Urbevilles* (this ed: Penguin Books, Middlesex, 1986)

Thomas Hood, *The Poetical Works* (London, n.d.)

Susan Kingsley Kent, *Gender and Power in Britain, 1640-1990* (Routledge, London and New York, 1999)

Jill Liddington and Jill Norris, *One hand tied behind us: The rise of the Women's Suffrage Movement* (Rivers Oram Press, London, New York, Sydney, 2000)

Elizabeth Longford, *A Pilgrimage of Passion: the life of Wilfrid Scawen Blunt* (Random House, New York, 1979)

Elizabeth Anne McCauley, *Industrial Madness: Commercial Photography in Paris 1848-871* (Yale University Press, New Haven and London, 1994)

Steven Marcus, *The Other Victorians: a study of sexuality and pornography in mid-nineteenth century England* (Book Club Associates, London, 1970)

Jan Marsh, *The Legend of Lizzie Siddal* (Quartet Books, London, 1989)

Jan Marsh, *Christina Rossetti: a literary biography* (Pimlico, London, 1994)

Michael Mason, *The Making of Victorian Sexuality* (Oxford University Press, Oxford, 1994)

Henry Mayhew, *Selections from London Labour and the London Poor* (this ed: Oxford University Press, Oxford, 1965)

David Newsome, *The Victorian World Picture: Perceptions and Introspections in an age of change* (HarperCollins, London, 1998)

ed. Clarissa Campbell Orr, *Women in the Victorian Art World* (Manchester University Press, Manchester, 1995)

Jane Robinson, *Unsuitable for Ladies: An anthology of women travellers* (Oxford University Press, Oxford, 1994)

Jane Robinson, *Angels of Albion: Women of the Indian Mutiny* (Penguin Books, London, 1997)

Alison Smith, *The Victorian Nude: Sexuality, morality and art* (Manchester University Press, Manchester, 1996)

'The Studio', *High art and low life: the Studio and the fin de siecle* (The Arthur M. Sackler Foundation, Washington DC, USA, 1993)

Alfred, Lord Tennyson, *Selected Poems* (Bloomsbury Poetry Classics, London, 1994)

Anthony Trollope, *The Way We Live Now* (this ed: Wordsworth Editions, Hertfordshire, 1995)

H.R.H. the Duchess of York, with Benita Stoney, *Victoria and Albert: Life at Osborne House* (Weidenfeld and Nicholson, London, 1991)

INDEX

ACKNOWLEDGEMENTS

With grateful thanks to the team at V&A Publications, particularly Slaney Begley for her adroit editing, Miranda Harrison for managing the project and Mary Wessel for her enthusiastic help with the picture research. Many thanks also to Steve Woodhouse in the V&A Picture Library.

I am very grateful to the staff of the Mary Evans Picture Library, working on behalf of the Fawcett Library, and the Archives of Royal Holloway and Bedford New College, both for their assistance with awkward enquiries; Paul Atterbury and Tessa Hore working on the V&A's 'Inventing New Britain' exhibition; and Buckinghamshire Chilterns University College for their support.

This book is dedicated to John Cooper, with fond thanks for his unflagging encouragement.